CREAMY MUSHROOM SAUCE

Preparation time: *10 minutes*
Total cooking time: *7 minutes*
Serves 4

meat or chicken (see below)
30 g butter
350 g button mushrooms, sliced
2 tablespoon white wine
½ cup chicken stock
½ cup cream
1 clove garlic, crushed
1 tablespoon chopped fresh chives

1. Pan-fry the meat or chicken of choice; remove from pan, cover with foil and keep warm. Melt the butter with the pan juices, add the mushrooms and stir over medium heat for 5 minutes or until soft and golden.
2. Add the wine, stock, cream and garlic and bring to the boil. Cook, uncovered, for 2 minutes, stirring constantly, until the sauce thickens slightly. Stir in the chives and serve immediately.

SERVE over pan-fried beef or veal steaks, or pan-fried chicken breast fillets.

TRADITIONAL GRAVY

Preparation time: *5 minutes*
Total cooking time: *5 minutes*
Serves 4-6

roast of choice (see below)
pan juices from roast
2 tablespoons plain flour
1 cup beef or chicken stock
salt and pepper

1. Remove the meat from the roasting pan and set aside. Place the pan on top of the stove. Sprinkle flour over the base of the pan and combine with the pan juices. Cook over medium heat for a minute or two while stirring constantly with a wooden spoon.
2. Add the stock gradually, scraping the bottom of the pan to dissolve any juices that may have become stuck. Make sure the stock and the flour mixture are well combined before adding more stock—this will stop the gravy becoming lumpy. Bring the gravy to the boil and cook for 1 minute, still stirring. Season to taste and serve immediately. (The gravy may be strained to remove any dark flecks or meat particles.)

SERVE with roast beef, lamb, chicken or pork.

Creamy Mushroom
Sauce (top) and
Traditional Gravy

RED WINE SAUCE

Preparation time: *5 minutes*
★ **Total cooking time:** *10 minutes*
Serves 4

meat of choice (see below)
30 g butter
1 small onion, thinly sliced
1 teaspoon plain flour
2 teaspoons soft brown sugar
¾ cup red wine
salt and freshly ground black pepper

1. Pan-fry meat; remove from pan, cover with foil, keep warm. Melt butter with pan juices, add onion; stir over medium heat 5 minutes or until very soft. Add flour and sugar.
2. Cook for 1 minute. Add wine gradually, stirring constantly. Bring to boil, reduce heat and simmer, stirring, for 5 minutes or until reduced by half. Season and serve.

SERVE over pan-fried beef steak or lamb cutlets.

MINT SAUCE

Preparation time: *5 minutes*
★ **Total cooking time:** *5 minutes*
Serves 6–8

¼ cup water
⅓ cup white sugar
2 tablespoons malt vinegar
⅓ cup finely chopped fresh mint

1. Combine water and sugar in a small pan. Stir over low heat without boiling until sugar dissolves. Bring to the boil; reduce heat and simmer for 3 minutes without stirring.
2. Remove the pan from the heat. Combine sugar mixture with vinegar and mint in a serving jug.

SERVE at room temperature with roast leg or rack of lamb.

BREAD SAUCE

Preparation time: *1 minute*
★ **Total cooking time:** *25 minutes*
Makes *1 cup*

2 whole cloves
1 medium onion, peeled
1 cup milk
1 bay leaf
50 g fresh breadcrumbs (3 slices)
¼ cup cream

1. Push cloves into onion. Combine onion, milk and bay leaf in pan. Bring to boil. Remove from heat, cover; leave to infuse 10 minutes. Remove onion and bay leaf.
2. Add breadcrumbs and season. Return pan to heat, cover; simmer gently for 10 minutes, stirring occasionally. Stir in cream. Serve.

SERVE warm with roast chicken or roast turkey.

From top: Red Wine Sauce,
Mint Sauce and Bread Sauce

SHIITAKE MUSHROOM SAUCE
Preparation time: 15 minutes
Total cooking time: 10 minutes
Serves 4-6

30 g butter
200 g shiitake mushrooms,
   thinly sliced
2 tablespoons muscat
¼ cup rich beef stock
2 tablespoons wholegrain mustard
¾ cup cream
salt and freshly ground pepper
1 tablespoon finely chopped
   fresh parsley

1. Melt the butter in a small pan, add the mushrooms and stir over moderate heat until the mushrooms are soft.
2. Add the muscat and stir until almost evaporated. Stir in the stock, mustard and cream, then bring to the boil while stirring. Lower the heat and simmer for 5 minutes or until the mixture has reduced and thickened slightly. Season, add parsely and serve.

SERVE over pan-fried, grilled or roast beef or pork, with grilled lamb cutlets, pan-fried tuna steaks, or chicken fillets, and beef or lamb burgers. Toss through hot pasta.

ANGEL SAUCE
Preparation time: 10 minutes
Total cooking time: 2 minutes
Serves 4

125 g butter
3 egg yolks
1½ tablespoons lemon juice
freshly ground white pepper
2 egg whites

1. Heat the butter slowly in a pan until it begins to bubble. Place the egg yolks, lemon juice and pepper in a blender and blend for 5 seconds. Slowly pour the hot butter onto the yolk mixture in a steady stream until all the butter has been added. Transfer the sauce to a large bowl and allow to cool. Stir occasionally to prevent a skin forming on the surface of the sauce.
2. Place the egg whites in a small, dry bowl. Using electric beaters, beat the whites until soft peaks form. Fold into the sauce. Refrigerate for at least 30 minutes before serving. (The sauce can be prepared ahead and refrigerated for up to 24 hours.)

SERVE over steamed artichokes, asparagus or green beans, cooked peeled prawns or grilled scallops, oysters on the half shell, smoked salmon or any grilled fish.

*Angel Sauce (top)
and Shiitake
Mushroom Sauce*

9

TOMATO PASTA SAUCE
■ *Preparation time:* 20 minutes
✳ *Total cooking time:* 20 minutes
Serves 4

1.5 kg large ripe tomatoes
1 tablespoon olive oil
1 medium onion, finely chopped
2 cloves garlic, crushed
1 teaspoon dried oregano leaves
2 tablespoons tomato paste
1 teaspoon sugar
salt and pepper

1. Mark a small cross on the base (opposite stem end) of each tomato. Place in boiling water for 2 minutes, remove with tongs and drain. Peel the skin down from the cross and discard. Finely chop the remaining tomato flesh.
2. Heat the oil in a medium pan. Add the onion and cook, stirring, over medium heat for 3 minutes or until soft. Add the garlic and cook for 1 minute. Add the tomato, oregano, tomato paste and sugar.
3. Bring to the boil, reduce the heat and simmer, uncovered, for about 15 minutes or until the sauce has thickened slightly. Season to taste. Keep, covered, for up to 2 days in the refrigerator, or freeze for up to 2 months. Reheat in a pan or in the microwave.

SERVE hot over pasta or with pan-fried beef steaks and veal schnitzel, or use as a pizza sauce.

RICH BOLOGNESE SAUCE
■ *Preparation time:* 15 minutes
✳ *Total cooking time:* 1½ hours
Serves 4

2 tablespoons olive oil
1 large onion, chopped
1 medium carrot, chopped
1 stick celery, chopped
2 cloves garlic, crushed
500 g beef mince
2 cups beef stock
1½ cups red wine
2 x 425 g canned tomatoes
1 teaspoon sugar

1. Heat oil in a large heavy based pan. Add onion, carrot and celery and cook, stirring, over medium heat for 5 minutes until softened. Add garlic and cook 1 minute further.
2. Add the mince to the pan. Cook, breaking up with a fork, until well browned. Add the stock, wine, undrained crushed tomatoes and the sugar.
3. Bring to the boil, reduce heat and simmer, uncovered, for 1–1½ hours, stirring occasionally. Season to taste with salt and pepper. Keep, covered, for up to 2 days in the refrigerator or freeze for up to 2 months. Reheat in a pan or in the microwave.

SERVE hot over pasta or as a sauce on a pizza base.

Rich Bolognese Sauce (top)
and Tomato Pasta Sauce

QUICK PEANUT SAUCE

★ *Preparation time:* 10 minutes
Total cooking time: 5 minutes
Makes about 1½ cups

1 cup pineapple juice
1 cup peanut butter
½ teaspoon garlic powder
½ teaspoon onion powder
2 tablespoons sweet chilli sauce
¼ cup soy sauce

1. Combine the pineapple juice, peanut butter, garlic powder, onion powder, chilli sauce and soy sauce in a small pan. Stir over medium heat until the mixture is smooth and heated through.
2. Add a little water for a thinner sauce, if preferred. This sauce will keep, covered, in the refrigerator for up to 3 days. Reheat in a pan over medium heat when required.

Serve with grilled or barbecued beef and chicken satay sticks.

CLASSIC SATAY SAUCE

★ *Preparation time:* 5 minutes
Total cooking time: 15 minutes
Makes 2 cups

1 cup roasted unsalted peanuts
2 tablespoons olive oil
1 onion, chopped
2 cloves garlic, crushed
3 cm piece green ginger, grated
½ teaspoon chilli powder
2 teaspoons curry powder
1 teaspoon ground cumin
400 ml can coconut milk
3 tablespoons soft brown sugar
1 tablespoon lemon juice
salt, to taste

1. Place the peanuts in a food processor and process until they are finely chopped.
2. Heat the oil in a medium pan. Add the onion and cook over medium heat for 5 minutes or until softened. Add the garlic, ginger, chilli, curry and cumin and cook, stirring, for 2 minutes.
3. Add the coconut milk, brown sugar and processed peanuts. Reduce the heat and cook for 5 minutes or until the sauce is thickened. Add the lemon juice, season and serve. (For a smoother sauce, process in a food processor for 30 seconds.)

Serve with beef or chicken kebabs and with grilled chicken.

Quick Peanut Sauce (top)
and Classic Satay Sauce

CHINESE LEMON SAUCE
- **Preparation time:** *10 minutes*
★ **Total cooking time:** *5 minutes*
Makes *1 cup*

¼ cup lemon juice
¼ cup chicken stock
½ cup water
1 tablespoon honey
1 tablespoon sugar
½ teaspoon grated ginger
1 tablespoon cornflour
1 tablespoon water
2 spring onions, sliced diagonally
pinch of salt

1. Combine the lemon juice, stock, water, honey, sugar and ginger in a small pan. Stir over medium heat until the sugar dissolves.
2. Increase the heat and bring the mixture to the boil. Combine the cornflour and water in a small bowl, add to the pan and allow to thicken. Remove from the heat, stir in the spring onions and season with salt.

SERVE warm over vegetables, spring rolls, pan-fried chicken or deep-fried fish.

SWEET AND SOUR SAUCE
- **Preparation time:** *10 minutes*
★ **Total cooking time:** *10 minutes*
Makes *1 cup*

2 tablespoons dry sherry
1 cup pineapple juice
3 tablespoons white wine vinegar
2 teaspoons soy sauce
2 tablespoons soft brown sugar
2 tablespoons tomato sauce
½ medium red capsicum, diced
1 tablespoon cornflour
1 tablespoon water

1. Combine the sherry, juice, vinegar, soy sauce, brown sugar and tomato sauce in a medium pan. Cook, stirring constantly, over low heat until the sugar is dissolved.
2. Bring to the boil and add the diced capsicum. Combine the cornflour and water in a small bowl. Add to the pan and cook, stirring constantly, until the mixture boils and thickens. Reduce the heat and simmer for 2 minutes. Serve at once.

SERVE with pan-fried, grilled or deep-fried fish, pan-fried pork or spring rolls.

Sweet & Sour Sauce (top) and Chinese Lemon Sauce

SPICED CRANBERRY SAUCE

Preparation time: 5 minutes
Total cooking time: 5 minutes
Makes 1 cup

250 g jar whole cranberry sauce
1 teaspoon grated orange rind
¼ cup orange juice
1 teaspoon ground ginger
½ teaspoon ground cardamom
¼ teaspoon ground allspice

1. Combine the cranberry sauce, rind, juice and spices in a small pan.
2. Bring the mixture to the boil over medium heat. Reduce the heat and simmer for 2 minutes.

SERVE at room temperature with turkey, chicken or pork.

APPLE SAUCE

Preparation time: 20 minutes
Total cooking time: 20 minutes
Makes 2 cups

6 green apples, peeled, cored
  and chopped
½ cup water
1 tablespoon lemon juice
1 tablespoon sugar
1 teaspoon finely grated lemon rind
¼ teaspoon cinnamon

1. Combine the apples, water and juice in a medium pan. Bring to the boil, reduce heat and simmer, covered, for 20 minutes or until apples are very soft. Cool.
2. Transfer the apple mixture to a food processor; add the sugar, rind and cinnamon. Process the mixture until smooth. Keep, covered, up to 3 days in the refrigerator.

SERVE either warm or at room temperature with pork or ham. Also good on pancakes or waffles.

CARAMELISED ONION SAUCE

Preparation time: 5 minutes
Total cooking time: 40 minutes
Makes 1½ cups

40 g butter
3 medium onions, sliced
1 tablespoon flour
1½ cups beef stock
1 tablespoon red wine vinegar

1. Melt the butter in a large pan. Add the onions and cook over low heat for 30 minutes or until soft and brown. Add the flour and cook, stirring constantly, for 1 minute.
2. Add the stock gradually, stirring constantly to combine. Add the vinegar, bring to the boil. Reduce heat; simmer for 2 minutes. Serve.

SERVE with steak or over sausages and hamburgers.

From top: Spiced
Cranberry Sauce, Apple
Sauce and Caramelised
Onion Sauce

MUSTARD SAUCE

Preparation time: 1 minute
Total cooking time: 15 minutes
Makes 1 cup

1 cup chicken stock
6 spring onions, finely chopped
1 tablespoon white wine vinegar
2 tablespoons wholegrain mustard
1 cup sour cream

1. Combine stock, onions, vinegar and mustard in a medium pan. Boil for 5 minutes or until the liquid is reduced by half. Add sour cream, stirring to combine. Heat through without boiling. Serve warm.

SERVE over pan-fried or grilled pork, lamb and veal.

FATHER'S FAVOURITE SAUCE

Preparation time: 15 minutes
Total cooking time: 40 minutes
Makes 2 cups

5 large ripe tomatoes (1 kg)
1 large onion
½ cup cider vinegar
1 cup soft brown sugar
¼ cup Worcestershire sauce
1 teaspoon ground allspice
½ teaspoon ground ginger
¼ teaspoon ground cloves
salt and pepper

1. Chop tomatoes and onion; place in large pan. Add other ingredients; bring to boil. Reduce heat; simmer 40 minutes, stirring occasionally.

Transfer to a bowl; cool. Place in food processor; process until almost smooth. Reheat to boiling, cool slightly; transfer to sterilised jars or bottles. Store in cool dark place for up to 6 months. Refrigerate after opening and use within 1 month.

SERVE with steak, chops, sausages, or as a relish with cold meats.

BARBECUE SAUCE

Preparation time: 15 minutes
Total cooking time: 6 minutes
Serves 6

2 teaspoons oil
1 small onion, finely chopped
1 tablespoon malt vinegar
1 tablespoon soft brown sugar
⅓ cup tomato sauce
1 tablespoon Worcestershire sauce

1. Heat oil in small pan. Cook onion over low heat for 3 minutes until soft, stirring occasionally. Add other ingredients, bring to boil. Reduce heat and simmer 3 minutes. Serve warm or at room temperature. Keeps in the refrigerator for 1 week.

SERVE with barbecued chops, steak, hamburgers or sausages.

From top: Mustard Sauce,
Barbecue Sauce and
Father's Favourite Sauce

TACO SAUCE

■ *Preparation time:* 10 minutes
★ *Total cooking time:* 20 minutes
Makes about 1 1/2 cups

1 tablespoon oil
1 small onion, finely chopped
1 teaspoon ground coriander
1 teaspoon ground cumin
1/2 teaspoon chilli powder
1 clove garlic, crushed
1 small red capsicum,
  finely chopped
1 small green capsicum,
  finely chopped
2 large ripe tomatoes,
  finely chopped
1/2 teaspoon sugar
salt and pepper

1. Heat the oil in a small pan. Add the onion and cook over medium heat for 2 minutes until soft. Add the spices and stir for 1 minute, then add the garlic and capsicum and stir-fry for 2 minutes.
2. Add the tomatoes and stir until combined. Bring to the boil, reduce heat, simmer 15 minutes, stirring occasionally, until thickened slightly. Add sugar and stir to combine; season. Store, covered, in the refrigerator for up to 3 days.

SERVE warm with tacos, nachos, or as a dip with cornchips.

From top: Taco Sauce,
Seafood Sauce and Dill Sauce

SEAFOOD COCKTAIL SAUCE

■ *Preparation time:* 10 minutes
★ *Total cooking time:* nil
Makes about 1 1/3 cups

3/4 cup mayonnaise
1/3 cup cream
2 teaspoons Worcestershire sauce
1/4 cup tomato sauce
Tabasco sauce
salt and white pepper

1. Place mayonnaise, cream and sauces in a small bowl; stir until combined. Add Tabasco and season to taste.

SERVE with any cooked, cold prawns or shellfish.

DILL SAUCE

■ *Preparation time:* 5 minutes
★ *Total cooking time:* nil
Makes 1 1/2 cups

1/2 cup yoghurt
1/2 cup sour cream
1 tablespoon horseradish cream
1/4 cup fresh dill, chopped
3 spring onions, finely chopped
salt and freshly ground
  black pepper

1. Combine yoghurt, sour cream and horseradish in a bowl and stir until creamy. Add dill and spring onions, mix well. Season, cover and chill.

SERVE with fish, or spoon over steamed new potatoes.

Hollandaise Sauce

A rich, golden sauce with a number of delicious variations—serve warm with poached or steamed chicken and fish, with egg dishes and with steamed or boiled vegetables.

BASIC HOLLANDAISE

■ Melt 175 g of butter in a small pan. Skim any froth from the top and discard; cool the melted butter. Combine 2 tablespoons of water and 4 egg yolks in a small pan. Using a wire whisk, beat for about 30 seconds until the mixture is pale and creamy. Place the pan over very low heat and continue whisking for 3 minutes until the mixture is thick and foamy; remove from the heat. (Make sure the pan does not get too hot or you will end up with scrambled eggs.) Add the cooled butter slowly, a little at a time at first, whisking well between each addition. Keep adding the butter in a thin stream, whisking continuously, until all the butter has been used. Try to avoid using the milky white whey in the bottom of the pan, but don't worry if a little gets in. Stir in 1 tablespoon lemon juice and season with salt and white pepper. Makes 1¼ cups.

ORANGE HOLLANDAISE (MALTAISE)

Replace the tablespoon of lemon juice with 2 tablespoons of orange juice. Strain the juice through a fine sieve to remove any pulp before measuring.

CHANTILLY HOLLANDAISE

Whip ½ cup of cream until soft peaks form. Using a metal spoon, fold into the hollandaise sauce and then adjust seasonings, to taste.

PROCESSOR METHOD

Use the same quantities as for the basic hollandaise, but place the yolks, water and juice in a food processor and blend for 10 seconds. Melt the butter; skim off the froth. With the motor running, add the melted hot butter to the processor in a thin stream. Transfer to a bowl and season to taste.

From left: Basic Hollandaise, Orange Hollandaise and Chantilly Hollandaise

White Sauces

Based on the famous French sauce, Béchamel, these creamy sauces are simple to make and delicious when served over vegetables, such as cauliflower or broccoli, or with fish or corned beef.

CLASSIC WHITE SAUCE (BECHAMEL)

Combine 1 cup of milk, a slice of onion, 1 bay leaf and 6 peppercorns in a small pan. Bring to the boil, remove from the heat and infuse for 10 minutes. Strain the milk and discard flavourings. Melt 30 g butter in a small pan and add 1 tablespoon plain flour. Cook, stirring, for 1 minute over medium heat until the mixture is golden and bubbling. Add the milk very slowly, a little at a time, and stir between each addition until the mixture is completely smooth. When all the milk has been added, keep stirring over medium heat until the mixture boils and thickens. Boil for 1 minute more and remove from the heat. Season with salt and white pepper. Makes 1 cup.

NOTE: Infusing the milk with onion, bay and peppercorns adds flavour to a plain white sauce. Plain milk may be used, particularly if the sauce is to have other flavourings.

From left: Classic White Sauce,
Cheese Sauce, Curry Sauce
and Parsley Sauce

CURRY SAUCE

■ Add a finely chopped small onion
and 2 teaspoons curry powder to
the melted butter and stir for
2 minutes until the onion is soft.
Add the flour and proceed with the
white sauce recipe as directed.

CHEESE SAUCE (MORNAY)

■ Make the white sauce as directed,
using 1⅓ cups milk. After
removing from the heat, add
½ cup finely grated tasty cheese and
¼ teaspoon mustard powder. Stir
until the cheese has melted and the
sauce is smooth. Season to taste.

PARSLEY SAUCE

■ Add ¼ cup finely chopped fresh
parsley to finished sauce and stir to
combine. Other fresh herbs such as
chives, dill or tarragon may be
added, or try a combination of
your favourite herbs.

Dipping Sauces

An essential part of Asian meals and tasty with deep-fried fish and seafood, dipping sauces are simple to prepare and add colour and interest to the table.

CUCUMBER SAUCE

- In a food processor combine half an unpeeled, roughly chopped Lebanese cucumber, half a peeled and chopped carrot, 2 roughly chopped spring onions, 1 seeded and chopped small red chilli, 1 teaspoon grated green ginger, 1 tablespoon roasted unsalted peanuts and 1 tablespoon chopped coriander. Process until finely chopped, being careful not to over-process. Place in a serving bowl. Heat 4 tablespoons caster sugar, ¾ cup white wine or rice vinegar and ¼ cup water in a small pan. Stir until dissolved and then pour over vegetables. Serve with Thai entrées such as spring rolls and fish cakes. Makes about 1½ cups.

GINGER SAUCE

- Combine 4 tablespoons grated ginger with 2 tablespoons peanut oil, 2 tablespoons sweet chilli sauce, 1 teaspoon caster sugar and 1 tablespoon chopped coriander in a small bowl. Serve with steamed or roasted chicken or duck or with any Chinese style dishes. Makes about ½ cup.

From left: Cucumber Sauce, Ginger Sauce and Thai Spicy

From left: Soy and Sesame Sauce, Coconut and Chilli Sauce and Japanese Sauce

COCONUT AND CHILLI SAUCE

Heat 2 teaspoons of oil in a small pan. Add 2 teaspoons curry paste and 1 small roughly chopped red chilli and stir for 30 seconds to heat through. Stir in ½ cup coconut milk, 1 teaspoon caster sugar, 1 teaspoon fish sauce and ¼ cup chopped basil leaves. Stir over low heat 2 minutes. Serve warm with deep-fried fish or seafood. Makes about ½ cup.

THAI SPICY SAUCE

Combine 2 finely chopped spring onions, 1 teaspoon chilli powder, 1 tablespoon lime or lemon juice, 1 tablespoon fish sauce and 1 teaspoon sugar in a glass or ceramic bowl. Serve with pork, beef or chicken Thai dishes. Makes about ¼ cup.

SOY AND SESAME SAUCE

Combine 1 cup rice or white wine vinegar and ½ cup caster sugar in a small pan. Stir over low heat until dissolved. Place in a serving bowl with 2 tablespoons dark soy sauce, ¼ teaspoon salt, 1 tablespoon toasted sesame seeds and 1 tablespoon honey. Serve with any Thai or Chinese entrées or with fried or steamed chicken or fish. Makes 1½ cups.

JAPANESE SAUCE

Combine ½ cup each of lemon juice and dark soy sauce in a screw-top jar. Add 1 tablespoon each of mirin and sake, 1 tablespoon dried bonito flakes and a 5 cm piece kombu seaweed. Refrigerate for 24 hours, then strain back into jar. Keeps 2 months, refrigerated. Use with sashimi and sushi. Makes 1¼ cups. (All ingredients are available from Asian food stores.)

DRESSINGS

As a final touch to salads, dressings are an essential part of a good cook's repertoire. This selection includes simple dressings of vinegar, oil and seasonings through to those with egg, cream or yoghurt.

THOUSAND ISLAND DRESSING

★ *Preparation time: 10 minutes*
Total cooking time: nil
Makes 2/3 cup

½ cup whole egg mayonnaise
1 tablespoon tomato paste
1 teaspoon French mustard
2 teaspoons malt vinegar
salt and white pepper

1. Place the mayonnaise, paste, mustard and vinegar in a small bowl. Stir until well combined and then season.
2. Cover and refrigerate for up to 3 days.

SERVED traditionally on lettuce leaves.

CAESAR DRESSING

★ *Preparation time: 10 minutes*
Total cooking time: 1 minute
Serves 6

1 egg
2 teaspoons white wine vinegar
3 teaspoon Dijon mustard
1 anchovy fillet
1 clove garlic, crushed
⅓ cup oil

1. Lower the egg into a pan of boiling water and cook for 1 minute; drain. Break into a small bowl and add the vinegar, mustard, anchovy and garlic, and then whisk to combine.
2. Add oil in a thin stream, whisking continuously, until the mixture is smooth and creamy. Keep, covered, in the refrigerator for up to 2 days.

SERVE on Caesar salad (cos lettuce, crisp bacon, croutons, shaved Parmesan). Also delicious on any green salad.

Thousand Island Dressing (above) and Caesar Dressing

WARM BACON DRESSING

★ ***Preparation time:*** *10 minutes*
Total cooking time: *5 minutes*
Serves *6*

3 slices bacon
1 tablespoon oil
2 tablespoons cider vinegar
2 teaspoons wholegrain mustard

1. Remove rind and fat from bacon. Cut bacon into thin strips. Heat oil in a pan and cook bacon until crisp.
2. Remove the pan from the heat and cool slightly. Add the vinegar and mustard and stir into the pan juices.

SERVE over boiled potatoes for a warm salad, or over a spinach salad.

BLUE CHEESE DRESSING

★ ***Preparation time:*** *5 minutes*
Total cooking time: *nil*
Makes about *1 cup*

½ cup whole egg mayonnaise
¼ cup thick cream
1 teaspoon white wine vinegar
1 tablespoon finely chopped chives
50 g blue cheese
salt and white pepper

1. Combine the mayonnaise, cream, wine vinegar and chopped chives in a small bowl.

From top: Warm Bacon Dressing,
Blue Cheese Dressing and
Mediterranean Dressing

2. Crumble the blue cheese into the mayonnaise mixture and gently stir through. Cover and refrigerate for up to 3 days.

SERVE over cooked asparagus, boiled small potatoes, on jacket potatoes or with a green salad.

MEDITERRANEAN LEMON DRESSING

★ ***Preparation time:*** *5 minutes*
Total cooking time: *nil*
Serves *6*

2 tablespoons chopped preserved
  lemon peel
1 small clove garlic, crushed
1 teaspoon honey, warmed
½ cup olive oil
1 tablespoon lemon juice
1 teaspoon chopped fresh oregano
  (or lemon thyme) leaves
2 tablespoons pine nuts
freshly ground pepper, to taste

1. Place the preserved peel, garlic and honey in food processor. Process until the lemon peel is finely chopped.
2. Add the oil, lemon juice, oregano and pine nuts and process until smooth. Season with pepper.

SERVE over cooked prawns, mussels, oysters on the shell, or grilled scallops. Also excellent with pan-fried salmon steaks.

Vinaigrettes

Based on oil and vinegar or lemon and often enhanced with herbs, mustard and other flavourings, vinaigrettes can add a tang and freshness to even the simplest green salad.

BASIC VINAIGRETTE (FRENCH DRESSING)

Place 2 tablespoons white wine vinegar, ⅓ cup light olive oil and 1 teaspoon French mustard in a small screw-top jar. Shake until the ingredients are combined. Season with salt and white pepper.

HERB VINAIGRETTE

Use a herb infused vinegar (see right) instead of plain vinegar in the basic recipe. Alternatively, add 1 tablespoon finely chopped fresh herbs to the basic recipe.

GARLIC AND LEMON VINAIGRETTE

Combine 2 tablespoons lemon juice, ⅓ cup vegetable oil and 1 teaspoon wholegrain mustard in a small screw-top jar. Add a whole peeled garlic clove and shake to combine. Leave for 30 minutes so that the flavours have time to combine. Remove the garlic clove and shake again before using. Season with salt and white pepper.

*From left: Basic Vinaigrette,
Herb Vinaigrette and
Garlic and Lemon Vinaigrette*

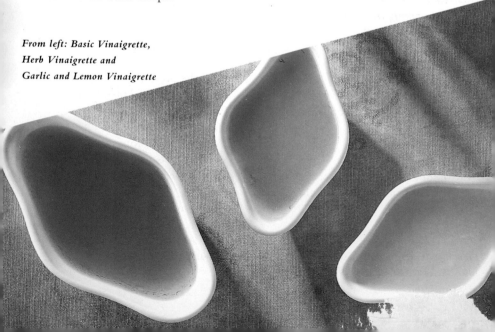

BALSAMIC VINAIGRETTE

Place 2 tablespoons balsamic vinegar and 1 teaspoon French mustard in a small bowl. Using a small wire whisk, beat in 1/3 cup of extra virgin olive oil, adding the oil slowly in a thin stream. Season with salt and pepper.

SESAME ORANGE DRESSING

Place 2 tablespoons orange juice and 1 teaspoon finely grated orange rind in a small screw-top jar. Add 1/3 cup vegetable oil and 1/4 teaspoon sesame oil. Shake well to combine and season with freshly ground black pepper.

HERB VINEGAR

Herb vinegars are available in most supermarkets and delicatessens. However, you can make your own by combining 1/4 cup fresh herbs (tarragon, dill, chives or basil) with 1 litre of white wine vinegar. Place in a sterilised bottle and leave for a week, shaking bottle occasionally. Strain and place in a clean sterilised bottle with a sprig of fresh herb.

From left: Balsamic Vinaigrette, Sesame Orange Dressing and Herb Vinegar

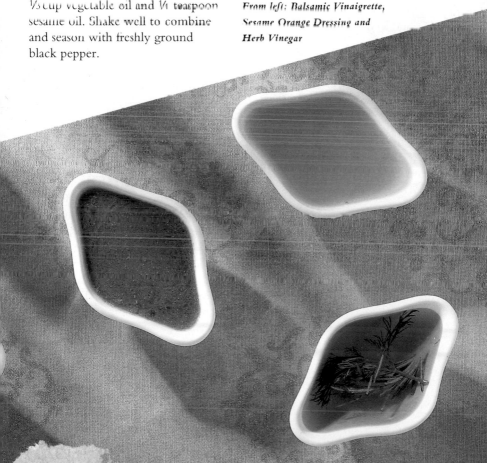

Mayonnaise

Used as a salad dressing or as a sauce, particularly with fish dishes, mayonnaise has many variations and is simple to make once you know how—see Secrets of Sauce-Making on page 59 for extra instructions.

BASIC MAYONNAISE

Place 2 egg yolks in a medium mixing bowl. Add 1 teaspoon Dijon mustard and 2 teaspoons lemon juice; whisk together for 30 seconds until light and creamy. Add 1 cup light olive oil, about a teaspoon at a time, whisking continuously. Increase the amount of oil as the mayonnaise thickens. When all the oil has been added, stir in an extra 2 teaspoons of lemon juice and season to taste with salt and white pepper. Makes about 1 cup.

PROCESSOR METHOD

Use the same ingredients as for basic mayonnaise, but place the yolks, mustard and juice in a food processor and process for 10 seconds. With the motor running, add the oil in a slow, thin stream until combined. Transfer to a bowl and season to taste.

Basic Mayonnaise (left),
Aïoli (top right),
Tartare Sauce (bottom left)
and Green Goddess
Dressing (bottom right)

AIOLI (GARLIC MAYONNAISE)

Crush 3 large cloves of garlic
and add to basic recipe in place
of the mustard.

TARTARE SAUCE

Make up 1 quantity of basic
mayonnaise. Add 2 finely chopped
spring onions, 2 tablespoons each
of chopped capers and gherkins,
1 tablespoon finely chopped
parsley and 2 teaspoons finely
chopped tarragon.

GREEN GODDESS DRESSING

Make up 1 quantity of basic
mayonnaise. Add 4 finely chopped
anchovy fillets, 1 clove crushed
garlic, 1/4 cup sour cream and
1/4 cup chopped fresh herbs.

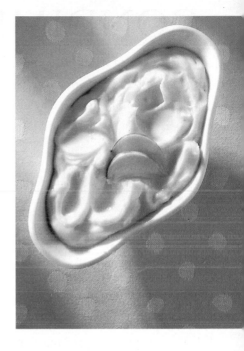

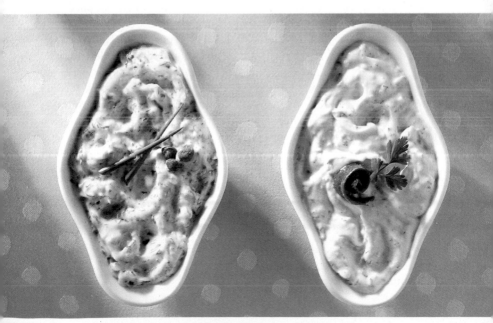

CONDIMENTS

Usually served as an accompaniment and including chutneys, relishes and salsas, condiments are often vegetable or fruit based and can liven up many simple dishes.

CORN RELISH

Preparation time: *5 minutes*
Total cooking time: *25 minutes*
Makes *2 cups*

1 cup white vinegar
¼ cup caster sugar
2 teaspoons dry mustard
1 small onion, finely chopped
425 g can corn kernels
¼ cup finely chopped
   red capsicum
1 teaspoon finely chopped red chilli
½ teaspoon turmeric
½ teaspoon salt
2 teaspoons cornflour
1 tablespoon water

1. Place vinegar, sugar and mustard in medium pan. Bring to boil, stirring until sugar dissolves. Reduce heat; simmer 5 minutes. Add onion, corn, capsicum, chilli, turmeric and salt. Cook until vegetables are tender.
2. Mix cornflour with water; add to mixture, stirring constantly. Cook 5 minutes to thicken. Spoon into warmed, sterilised jars; seal while hot and store in a cool, dark place.

SERVE with cold meats or on jacket potatoes.

MANGO CHUTNEY

Preparation time: *15 minutes*
Total cooking time: *1 hour*
   10 minutes
Makes *3 cups*

3 large mangoes
1 teaspoon salt
1 cup white vinegar
1½ cups raw sugar
2 small red chillies, seeded
   and chopped
5 cm fresh ginger, grated
½ cup dates, finely chopped

1. Peel the mangoes, remove stones and chop flesh; sprinkle with salt.
2. Place vinegar and sugar in a large pan and bring to the boil. Reduce heat and simmer for 5 minutes.
3. Add the mango, chillies, ginger and dates. Simmer for 1 hour or until the mango is tender. Pour into warm sterilised jars and seal. Store in a cool, dark place.

SERVE with curries, ham sandwiches, sausages or on cold meats.

Corn Relish (top) and
Mango Chutney

EGGPLANT RELISH

Preparation time: *15 minutes plus*
standing time
Total cooking time: *15 minutes*
Makes about *1 1/2 cups*

300 g baby eggplant, cut into
    5 mm slices
salt
2 tablespoons olive oil
1 medium red onion,
    finely chopped
1–2 cloves garlic, crushed
1 tablespoon soft brown sugar
2 tablespoons balsamic vinegar
1 tablespoon olive oil, extra
¼ cup chopped fresh parsley

1. Place the eggplant in a colander
   and sprinkle with salt. Set aside for
   20 minutes.
2. Meanwhile, heat 1 tablespoon of
   the oil in a medium frying pan.
   Cook the onion and garlic over
   medium heat, stirring frequently,
   for 8 minutes or until the onion is
   softened. Remove with a slotted
   spoon and place in a glass or
   ceramic bowl.
3. Wash the eggplant, drain and pat
   dry with paper towels. Heat the
   remaining oil in a pan; add the
   eggplant and cook, stirring, over
   medium–high heat for 2 minutes.
   Reduce the heat and cook, stirring

frequently, for 5 minutes, or until
the eggplant is softened and
cooked. Do not allow to burn.
4. Add the eggplant to the onion
   mixture and stir in the sugar,
   vinegar, extra oil and parsley.
   Cover with plastic wrap and set
   aside at room temperature for
   30 minutes. Will keep for 4 days,
   covered and refrigerated, but is best
   served at room temperature.

SERVE with barbecued, grilled
or roast meats such as lamb,
beef or kangaroo. Use as a
bruschetta topping, with meat
as a focaccia filling or as a side
dish with cold meats.

HORSERADISH CREAM

Preparation time: *5 minutes*
Total cooking time: *nil*
Makes *2/3 cup*

⅓ cup bottled horseradish
¼ cup sour cream
1 tablespoon snipped fresh
    chives
salt and pepper

1. Combine the horseradish and sour
   cream in a small bowl, beating
   until well mixed.
2. Fold in the chives and season to
   taste with salt and pepper.

SERVE with vegetable crudités,
salads, smoked fish or over savoury
foods such as fish cakes.

Eggplant Relish (top)
and Horseradish Cream

Harissa

Preparation time: *10 minutes*
Total cooking time: *20 minutes*
Serves 6

100 g dried whole red chillies
6 cloves garlic, crushed
1/3 cup salt
1/3 cup ground coriander
1/3 cup ground cumin
2/3 cup olive oil

1. Remove the stems from the chillies. Cut in half lengthways, then remove and discard the seeds. Cover with boiling water and set aside to soften for 5 minutes.
2. Drain the chillies and combine with the garlic, salt and spices in a food processor. With the motor running, add the oil in a thin stream until the mixture is well combined. Keep the sauce, covered, in the refrigerator for up to 2 weeks. Serve at room temperature as an accompaniment.

SERVE with Moroccan foods such as couscous, or stir into soups and stews for extra spice.

Tomato relish

Preparation time: *15 minutes*
Total cooking time: *1 hour 10 minutes*
Makes 4 cups

1.5 kg tomatoes, roughly chopped
3 large onions, chopped
2 cups soft brown sugar
2 cups tarragon vinegar
2 cloves garlic, crushed
2 teaspoons dried basil
1 tablespoon dried mustard
1 tablespoon curry powder
1 teaspoon ground allspice

1. Combine all the ingredients in a large pan. Bring the mixture slowly to the boil, stirring constantly until the sugar dissolves.
2. Reduce the heat and simmer for 1 hour, stirring occasionally, until the mixture is thick. Spoon into warm sterilised jars, and seal while the mixture is still hot. Store in a cool, dark place.

SERVE with cheese and biscuits, roasts, cold meats, hamburgers or ploughman's lunch.

*Harissa (top) and
Tomato Relish*

FRUIT CHUTNEY

★ **Preparation time:** *15 minutes*
Total cooking time: *1 hour*
  15 minutes
Makes *5 cups*

500 g green apples
500 g pears
2 onions, chopped
½ cup sultanas
¼ cup currants
1 cup soft brown sugar
2 cloves garlic, chopped
3 cups cider vinegar
1 teaspoon five spice powder
1 teaspoon mixed spice
¼ cup tomato paste

1. Peel core and dice the apples and pears. Combine apple, pears, onions, sultanas, currants, sugar, garlic, vinegar, spices and tomato paste in a large, heavy-based pan.
2. Bring the mixture to the boil over medium heat. Reduce the heat and simmer gently for 1 hour, stirring occasionally, until the fruit is tender.
3. Spoon into warmed and sterilised jars and seal while still hot. Store in a cool, dark place.

Serve with cold meats, cheese or sausages.

CHILLI JAM

★ **Preparation time:** *25 minutes*
★ **Total cooking time:** *30 minutes*
Makes *1 cup*

12 red jalapeno chillies
2 medium ripe tomatoes
1 small onion, finely chopped
1 green apple, finely grated
½ cup red wine vinegar
½ cup sugar

1. Cut the chillies in half lengthways, then remove and discard seeds. Lay, cut side down, on an oven tray and place under a hot grill until the skin is black. Cover with foil and leave to cool.
2. Cut a small cross in the base (opposite stem end) of the tomatoes, cover with boiling water and leave for 2 minutes. Drain and cool. Peel the skin from the chillies and tomatoes and chop the flesh finely.
3. Combine the onion, apple, vinegar and sugar with the tomato and chilli in a medium pan. Stir until sugar has dissolved and bring to the boil. Reduce heat and simmer for 30 minutes. Keep, covered, in the refrigerator for up to a month.

Note: Use sparingly as a relish with cheese or cold meat, or add to soups and stews for extra heat.

Fruit Chutney (top)
a   *Chilli Jam*

Pesto Sauces

A thick uncooked sauce, traditionally made with basil, pine nuts and Parmesan cheese and served with pasta, pesto is also delicious when made with other herbs and vegetables.

BASIL PESTO

Wash and dry 2 bunches of basil leaves. Place in food processor with ⅓ cup toasted pine nuts, 2 cloves crushed garlic and ⅓ cup finely grated Parmesan cheese. Process until finely chopped; with motor running, add ⅓ cup of olive oil in a thin stream until well combined. Season with salt and pepper.

PARSLEY PESTO

Wash and dry leaves of 2 bunches of parsley. Place in a food processor and add 2 tablespoons lemon juice, 1 clove crushed garlic and ½ cup toasted blanched almonds; process until finely chopped. With the motor running, add ⅓ cup light olive oil in a thin stream until mixture is well combined.

**Basil Pesto (left) and
Parsley Pesto**

ROCKET PESTO

- Wash and dry leaves of 2 bunches of rocket. Place in a food processor with 1–2 cloves crushed garlic, ½ cup toasted macadamia nuts and ½ cup finely grated Parmesan or pecorino cheese. Process until finely chopped. With the motor running, add ½ cup extra virgin olive oil in a thin stream until thick and creamy. Season to taste.

CORIANDER PESTO

- Trim the roots from 2 bunches of coriander, leaving most of the stem. Wash and dry stems and place in a food processor with 2 cloves crushed garlic, ⅓ cup toasted macadamia nuts and 1 teaspoon chopped chilli. Process until finely chopped. With motor running, add ⅓ cup olive oil in a thin stream until well combined. Season.

SUN-DRIED TOMATO PESTO

- Soak 1 cup of dried tomatoes in boiling water for a few minutes until soft. Drain and squeeze out excess water. Place in a food processor with 1 clove crushed garlic and ¼ cup each of walnuts and Parmesan cheese. Process until finely chopped. With the motor running, add ⅓ cup olive oil in a thin stream until well combined. Season with salt and pepper.

Rocket Pesto (top), Coriander Pesto (bottom left) and Sun-Dried Tomato Pesto (right)

Butters

Using a flavoured butter is one of the simplest ways to spice up a wide variety of foods. Roll the prepared butter into a log shape and cover in plastic wrap. Refrigerate until firm and then cut into slices.

BLUE CHEESE SPREAD
- Combine 200 g blue cheese, 125 g butter, ¼ cup chopped parsley and 1 teaspoon lemon juice in a food processor. Process for 30 seconds or until well mixed.

ANCHOVY BUTTER
- Using electric beaters, beat 125 g softened butter with 4 finely chopped anchovy fillets, 1 tablespoon lemon juice and 1 tablespoon finely chopped fresh parsley in a small bowl until well combined.

From left: Tangy Mustard Butter, Garlic and Herb Butter and Curry Spread

*From left: Blue Cheese Spread
and Anchovy Butter*

GARLIC AND HERB BUTTER

Using electric beaters, beat 2 cloves of crushed garlic with 125 g soft butter and 2 tablespoons chopped fresh herbs in a small bowl until well combined.

CURRY SPREAD

Place 2 teaspoons curry powder in a dry frying pan and cook over medium heat for about 1 minute or until fragrant. Transfer to a small bowl and allow to cool, and then add 125 g butter. Using electric beaters, beat until the mixture is evenly combined.

TANGY MUSTARD BUTTER

Using electric beaters, beat 125 g softened butter with 2 teaspoons finely grated lemon rind, 1 tablespoon lemon juice and 1 tablespoon wholegrain mustard in a small bowl until well combined.

Curry Coolers

Simple to make, colourful on the table and usually prepared well ahead of time, these coolers are essential accompaniments to spicy food and a delight for the curry lover.

Coconut bananas

- Peel 2 large bananas and cut into thick slices. Dip slices into ⅓ cup lemon juice, then toss in enough desiccated coconut to coat each piece. Serve at room temperature.

Cucumber raita

- Combine 2 peeled, finely chopped Lebanese cucumbers with 1 cup of plain yoghurt. Fry 1 teaspoon ground cumin in a dry pan for a minute until fragrant, then add to yoghurt mixture with ½ teaspoon grated ginger. Season with salt and freshly ground black pepper. Place in a serving bowl and dust with some paprika to garnish. Serve chilled.

*Coconut Bananas (top)
and Cucumber Raita*

FRESH TOMATO RELISH

Finely chop 1 medium tomato and a small onion. Combine with 2 tablespoons finely chopped fresh mint leaves and 1 tablespoon lemon juice. Add 1 teaspoon sugar, and season with salt and pepper. Serve chilled.

CORIANDER CHUTNEY

Wash, dry and roughly chop 1 whole bunch of coriander, including roots. Place in a food processor with ¼ cup desiccated coconut, 1 tablespoon soft brown sugar, 1 teaspoon salt, 1 tablespoon grated fresh ginger, 1 small chopped onion and 2 tablespoons lemon juice. Remove the seeds from 1-2 small green chillies. Roughly chop the chillies and add to bowl; process for about 1 minute or until finely chopped. Serve chilled.

CREAMY MINT COOLER

Combine ½ cup cream with ½ cup plain yoghurt. Add ¼ cup chopped mint leaves and a pinch of cayenne pepper. Serve chilled.

From top: Fresh Tomato Relish, Coriander Chutney and Creamy Mint Cooler

Salsas

Highly seasoned, often with chilli, these spicy accompaniments are traditionally served with Mexican meals and are also excellent with barbecued or cold meats and vegetables.

PEACH SALSA

Peel and chop 2 firm yellow peaches into 1 cm cubes. Place 1 tablespoon lime juice, 2 teaspoons fish sauce (nam pla) and 1–2 teaspoons sweet chilli sauce in a medium bowl; mix well. Add peaches, 1 finely chopped small red onion, 1 tablespoon chopped mint and 1 tablespoon chopped coriander. Toss gently to combine. Cover and refrigerate for 30 minutes, and then serve. Serves 4.

GRILLED TOMATO SALSA

Heat grill. Cut 4 large vine-ripened tomatoes in half, remove or squeeze out seeds. Place on foil, cut side down, under grill. Grill until skin is blistered and loose. Peel off skin, cool and then chop flesh. Combine tomato, ½ finely chopped red onion, 1–2 crushed garlic cloves, 1–2 seeded and finely chopped small red or green chillies, ¼ cup chopped fresh coriander, 1 tablespoon olive oil, 1 tablespoon lime or lemon juice, salt and freshly ground black pepper in a glass or ceramic bowl. Leave to stand at room temperature for at least an hour. Makes 1¼ cups.

RED CAPSICUM SALSA

Heat grill. Place 2 red capsicum, quartered lengthways and seeded, skin side up on a foil-lined tray. Brush skin lightly with oil. Grill capsicum for 8–10 minutes until skin is blistered and blackened, taking care not to burn the flesh. Remove from heat and place in a paper or plastic bag, leave for 10 minutes. Meanwhile, place 1 red onion, peeled and sliced into 1 cm rings, and 1–2 unpeeled cloves of garlic on grill tray. Turn and grill for 5 minutes, or until onion and garlic are slightly softened. (Make sure they do not burn or the flavour will be bitter.) Remove skin from grilled capsicum and chop flesh roughly. Chop grilled onion slices roughly and peel garlic cloves. Place capsicum, onion, garlic, and 1–2 small red chillies in food processor. Process until ingredients are well chopped but not mushy. Place in a glass or ceramic bowl. Stir in 2 tablespoons olive oil, ¼ cup chopped basil, 1 teaspoon grated lemon rind, 1 tablespoon red wine vinegar or balsamic vinegar and salt and freshly ground black pepper. Makes about 1½ cups.

MANGO AND MINT SALSA

In a glass or ceramic bowl, combine the chopped flesh of 2 ripe mangoes, 3 finely chopped spring onions, ½ cup chopped mint, 1 tablespoon lime or lemon juice, and some freshly ground black pepper. Cover the bowl with plastic wrap and set aside for a minimum of 15 minutes before serving at room temperature. Keeps well, covered, and refrigerated, for up to a day. Makes about 1½ cups.

Note: Use canned mangoes if fresh ones are out of season. The results will be satisfactory, although not as tasty as when fresh mangoes are used.

From left: Peach Salsa,
Grilled Tomato Salsa,
Red Capsicum Salsa
and (above) Mango and
Mint Salsa

SWEET SAUCES

Dressing up simple desserts such as ice cream, fresh or poached fruit, pancakes and steamed puddings is made very easy with the addition of these luscious sweet sauces.

HOT CHOCOLATE SAUCE

Preparation time: *5 minutes*
Total cooking time: *20 minutes*
Makes *about 1 1/4 cups*

200 g dark chocolate, chopped
3/4 cup water
1 tablespoon caster sugar
1/2 teaspoon vanilla essence
1/4 cup cream
1 teaspoon butter
1 tablespoon rum or brandy,
    optional

1. Place the chocolate, water and sugar in the top of a double boiler. Place over low heat and simmer until the chocolate has melted. Leave to simmer for 15 minutes, stirring occasionally.
2. Remove from the heat and stir in the vanilla, cream, butter and optional rum or brandy. Serve immediately. Store for up to 2 weeks in a screw-top jar. The sauce will thicken on refrigeration, but can be reheated gently to serve.

SERVE hot over ice cream or as a sauce for profiteroles, waffles and pancakes.

BRANDY CREAM SAUCE

Preparation time: *10 minutes*
Total cooking time: *nil*
Serves *8*

2 egg yolks
1/3 cup caster sugar
1/3 cup brandy
1 cup cream, whipped
2 egg whites

1. Place the egg yolks and sugar in a small bowl. Using electric beaters, beat until the mixture is thick and creamy and the sugar is dissolved. Transfer to a large bowl. Stir in the brandy and fold in the whipped cream. (Whisky or calvados may be used instead of brandy.)
2. Place the egg whites in a small dry bowl. Using electric beaters, beat until soft peaks form. Fold into the yolk mixture. Serve immediately.

SERVE with fresh or poached fruit or with steamed plum or chocolate pudding.

Hot Chocolate Sauce (top)
and Brandy Cream Sauce

MOCHA SAUCE

Preparation time: 10 minutes
Total cooking time: 5 minutes
Makes 2 cups

60 g butter
150 g dark chocolate, chopped
1½ cups cream
1 tablespoon instant coffee powder
2 tablespoons crème de cacao
  (optional)

1. Combine the butter, chocolate, cream and coffee powder in a pan. Stir over low heat until the butter and chocolate have melted and the mixture is smooth.
2. Remove from heat; stir in crème de cacao, if using. Serve warm.

SERVE with vanilla or chocolate pudding and with ice cream.

MUSCAT CREAM

Preparation time: 7 minutes plus
  refrigeration time
Total cooking time: nil
Makes about 2 cups

300 ml sour cream
¼ cup soft brown sugar
1 egg yolk
2 tablespoons muscat liqueur

From top: Mocha Sauce,
Muscat Sauce and
Crème Anglaise

1. Place the sour cream, brown sugar and egg yolk in a medium bowl. Using electric beaters, beat for 5 minutes or until thick and glossy.
2. Beat in the muscat. Cover and refrigerate for a minimum of 2 hours. Keeps for up to 3 days.

SERVE in place of beaten cream. Serve with warm pastries, fruit tarts, hot or cold puddings and fresh or cooked fruit.

CREME ANGLAISE

Preparation time: 10 minutes
Total cooking time: 5 minutes
Serves 4-6

3 egg yolks
2 tablespoons caster sugar
1½ cups milk
½ teaspoon vanilla essence

1. Whisk the yolks and sugar in a bowl for 2 minutes until light and creamy. Heat the milk in a small pan until almost boiling; pour onto egg mixture, stirring constantly.
2. Return the mixture to the pan and stir over low heat for about 5 minutes until slightly thickened. Do not boil or the custard will curdle. Remove from heat, stir in essence and transfer to a jug to serve. Best made 30 minutes before serving. Cover surface with plastic wrap to avoid a skin forming.

SERVE as you would any custard with poached fruit and puddings.

BUTTERSCOTCH SAUCE

Preparation time: 5 minutes
Total cooking time: 15 minutes
Makes about 1½ cups

125 g butter
½ cup soft brown sugar
2 tablespoons golden syrup
½ cup cream
1 teaspoon vanilla essence

1. Combine the butter and sugar in a medium pan. Stir over low heat until the butter has melted and the sugar has dissolved. Bring to the boil.

2. Add golden syrup and cream. Reduce heat and simmer for 10 minutes or until the sauce is slightly thickened. Remove from the heat and add the vanilla. Serve hot or cold. The mixture will thicken on standing.

SERVE spooned over ice cream and with waffles or pancakes.

BERRY COULIS

Preparation time: 8 minutes
Total cooking time: nil
Makes about 1–1½ cups

250 g strawberries, raspberries or blackberries
2–4 tablespoons icing sugar, or to taste
1 tablespoon lemon juice
1–2 tablespoons Cointreau or Grand Marnier, optional

1. Hull strawberries. Place the berries in a blender or food processor. Add the icing sugar and lemon juice and blend or process until smooth.

2. Add Cointreau or Grand Marnier, to taste. Will keep, covered and refrigerated, for up to 3 days.

SERVE with fresh and cooked whole fruit, gelatine desserts, soufflés and ice cream.

Note: Use fresh or frozen fruit; frozen berries are often available in supermarkets. Sieve the fruit if a smooth sauce is required.
For variety make Mango Coulis: use 2 mangoes, peeled, seeded and pureed or frozen mango puree. Proceed as above.

Butterscotch Sauce (top)
and Berry Coulis

SECRETS OF SAUCE-MAKING

Whipping up a sauce is the easiest way to turn ordinary food into something special. Most sauce recipes are simply a matter of combining a few ingredients, although some of the classic sauces involve techniques which must be followed closely. This is not to say that they are difficult to make, but the following points will help you make perfect sauces every time.

Try to use heavy-based stainless steel pans for sauce-making, but if you must use an aluminium pan only use a wooden spoon as your stirring tool. A metal spoon or whisk in an aluminium pan will discolour the sauce. Heavy-based stainless steel pans distribute the heat more evenly and are less likely to 'catch' or burn on the bottom.

Cook the butter and flour mixture for about a minute. (White Sauce)

Stir the mixture until completely smooth between each addition of milk. (White Sauce)

WHITE SAUCE: White sauce should be a part of every cook's repertoire but 'fear of lumps' can be a deterrent. The butter and flour mixture, which is known as the *roux*, must be cooked for a full minute to remove the raw taste from the flour. The milk is then added a little at a time, and stirred to a smooth paste between each addition. You can add the milk a little faster as you come to the end, but all lumps must be stirred out before adding more milk or they will be impossible to get rid of later. If the sauce needs to stand for a short time before use, cover with a sheet of plastic wrap placed directly on the surface of the sauce to prevent a skin forming.

HOLLANDAISE SAUCE: Making Hollandaise is another task which can appear daunting but it is easy when you know how. Hollandaise, like mayonnaise, is what is known as an emulsified sauce. That is, you

To clarify, skim the froth from the top of the butter. (Hollandaise)

Add the butter gradually to the whisked yolks. (Hollandaise)

must create an emulsion where all the ingredients are combined correctly to the desired thickness and do not separate on standing. It sounds complicated but gets easier with practice. The butter used in the sauce is clarified, which means it is melted and the solids, both the foam on top of the melted butter and the whey in the bottom of the pan, are discarded. Using clarified butter contributes to a smoother sauce. The egg yolks are whisked with the water in a pan over very low heat until thick and foamy, and then removed from the heat. This creates a stable base for the sauce. The butter is added very slowly to the egg yolks, while whisking continuously, to emulsify mixture. To make the Hollandaise in a food processor, the eggs are whisked in the machine, then the hot butter is added to create the emulsion.

MAYONNAISE: Mayonnaise employs the same principles used in Hollandaise. First whisk the yolks, mustard and juice thoroughly in a bowl to create the base, and then add the oil almost drop by drop at first, slowly increasing to a thin stream while whisking constantly. Stand the bowl on a damp cloth to prevent it slipping while whisking. Mayonnaise may also be made in the food processor.

Add the oil drop by drop to the whisked yolks, mustard and juice. (Mayonnaise)

Pour the oil in a thin stream into the processor with the motor running (Mayonnaise)

59

SAUCES FOR COURSES

COURSE	SAUCES

BEEF

PAN-FRIED STEAK	Green Peppercorn, Béarnaise, Shiitake Mushroom, Red Wine, Creamy Mushroom, Tomato Pasta, Caramelised Onion, Father's Favourite, Eggplant Relish, all flavoured butters
GRILLED OR BARBECUED	Béarnaise, Shiitake Mushroom, Tomato Pasta, Caramelised Onion, Father's Favourite, Barbecue, all flavoured butters
ROAST	Béarnaise, Traditional Gravy, Shiitake Mushroom, Caramelised Onion, Eggplant Relish, Horseradish Cream
BARBECUED	Shiitake Mushroom, Tomato Pasta, Satay, Quick Peanut, Caramelised Onion, Father's Favourite, Barbecue, Grilled Tomato Salsa, Red Capsicum Salsa, all flavoured butters
CORNED BEEF	White, Parsley
COLD MEATS	Father's Favourite, Apple Sauce, Eggplant Relish, Horseradish Cream, Fruit Chutney, Mango Chutney, Corn Relish, Peach Salsa, Tomato Relish, Chilli Jam
SAUSAGES	Curry, Caramelised Onion, Father's Favourite, Barbecue, Mango Chutney, Tomato Relish, Fruit Chutney
HAMBURGERS	Shiitake Mushroom, Satay, Quick Peanut, Caramelised Onion, Taco, Father's Favourite, Barbecue, Eggplant Relish, Horseradish Cream, Tomato Relish, Chilli Jam, Peach Salsa, Grilled Tomato Salsa, Red Capsicum Salsa, Mayonnaise

LAMB

PAN-FRIED CUTLETS, CHOPS OR FILLETS	Red Wine, Mint, Shiitake Mushroom, Father's Favourite, Eggplant Relish, Tomato Relish
GRILLED CUTLETS, CHOPS	Shiitake Mushroom, Mustard
BARBECUED	Grilled Tomato Salsa, Red Capsicum Salsa
ROAST	Traditional Gravy, Mint

COURSE	SAUCES

PORK

PAN-FRIED STEAK, FILLETS OR CHOPS
: Shiitake Mushroom, Chinese Lemon, Sweet and Sour, Spiced Cranberry, Mustard, Apple Sauce, Peach Salsa, Mango and Mint Salsa, Tangy Mustard Butter

GRILLED CHOPS
: Shiitake Mushroom, Apple Sauce, Mustard

BARBECUED
: Peach Salsa, Mango and Mint Salsa, Tangy Mustard Butter

ROAST
: Shiitake Mushroom, Traditional Gravy, Spiced Cranberry, Apple Sauce

VEAL

PAN-FRIED STEAKS/SCHNITZEL
: Tomato Pasta, Angel, Creamy Mushroom, Mustard

CHICKEN/TURKEY

PAN-FRIED BREAST FILLETS
: Green Peppercorn, Shiitake Mushroom, Tomato, Creamy Mushroom, Chinese Lemon, Sweet and Sour, Spiced Cranberry

ROAST
: Gravy, Bread, Spiced Cranberry

BARBECUED
: Shiitake Mushroom, Tomato, Satay, Quick Peanut, Chinese Lemon, Sweet and Sour, Peach Salsa, Grilled Tomato, Red Capsicum Salsa

GAME
: Gravy, Red Wine, Caramelised Onion

FISH

SHELLFISH

PRAWNS, LOBSTER, CRAB
: Angel, Seafood Cocktail, Thousand Island Dressing, Mediterranean Lemon Dressing, Green Goddess Dressing

OYSTERS, MUSSELS,
: White, Cheese, Tomato, Angel

SCALLOPS
: Seafood Cocktail, Thousand Island Dressing, Mediterranean Lemon Dressing

COURSE	SAUCES
SALMON	
PAN-FRIED STEAKS	Béarnaise, Angel, Dill, Mediterranean Lemon Dressing, Peach Salsa, Mango and Mint Salsa
POACHED WHOLE OR FILLETS	Béarnaise, Angel
TROUT	
SMOKED	Horseradish Cream
TUNA	
PAN-FRIED OR BARBECUED STEAKS	Shiitake Mushroom, Olive Tomato, all salsas
WHITE FILLETS	
PAN-FRIED, GRILLED	Angel, Sweet and Sour, Dill
GRILLED OR BARBECUED	Tomato Salsa, Red Capsicum, Mango and Mint
DEEP-FRIED (CRUMBED OR BATTERED)	Chinese Lemon, Sweet and Sour Tartare
WHOLE FISH	
BAKED, PAN-FRIED OR BARBECUED	Chinese Lemon, Sweet and Sour, Dill
SMOKED FISH	
HADDOCK, KIPPERS	White, Parsley, Cheese

VEGETABLES

ARTICHOKES	Angel, Hollandaise, Mayonnaise, Aïoli
ASPARAGUS	Angel, Hollandaise, Orange Hollandaise, Mayonnaise, Aïoli
BEANS (GREEN)	Angel
BROCCOLI	White, Cheese
CAULIFLOWER	White, Cheese

COURSE	SAUCES
POTATOES	Dill, Blue Cheese Dressing, Corn Relish, Aïoli
TOMATOES	Vinaigrette, Herb Vinaigrette, Garlic and Lemon Vinaigrette, Balsamic Vinaigrette

SALADS

ASIAN STYLE	Sesame Orange Dressing
AVOCADO	All vinaigrettes, Peach Salsa
CAESAR	Caesar Dressing
CHICKEN	Mediterranean Lemon Dressing, Mayonnaise
EGG	Mayonnaise
GREEN LEAF	Thousand Island, all vinaigrettes, Blue Cheese Dressing, Mediterranean Lemon Dressing
PASTA	Garlic and Lemon Vinaigrette, Sesame Orange Dressing, Mayonnaise
POTATO	Dill, Warm Bacon Dressing, all vinaigrettes, Mayonnaise
SPINACH	Sesame Orange Dressing, Warm Bacon Dressing

PASTA

Shiitake Mushroom, Tomato Pasta, Rich Bolognese, Grilled Tomato Salsa, Red Capsicum Salsa, all Pestos

SWEETS

FRESH FRUIT	Brandy Cream, Muscat Cream, Berry Coulis
POACHED FRUIT	Brandy Cream, Muscat Cream, Crème Anglaise, Berry Coulis
ICE CREAM	Hot Chocolate, Mocha, Butterscotch, Berry Coulis
PANCAKES/WAFFLES	Hot Chocolate, Butterscotch, Berry Coulis, Apple Sauce
STEAMED/BAKED PUDDINGS	Brandy Cream, Crème Anglaise, Mocha
FRUIT PIES & TARTS	Muscat Cream, Crème Anglaise

INDEX